Sons of Temperance of North America

Blue Book for the Use of Subordinate Divisions

of the order of the Sons of Temperenance

Sons of Temperance of North America

Blue Book for the Use of Subordinate Divisions
of the order of the Sons of Temperenance

ISBN/EAN: 9783337891466

Printed in Europe, USA, Canada, Australia, Japan

Cover: Foto ©Andreas Hilbeck / pixelio.de

More available books at **www.hansebooks.com**

BLUE BOOK

FOR THE USE OF

SUBORDINATE DIVISIONS,

OF THE ORDER OF THE

SONS OF TEMPERANCE.

No part of the Blue Book shall be altered or printed, except at the expressed direction of the National Division. Any Officer or Brother who shall retain the same, in whole or in part, after the expiration of his term of service, or who shall directly or indirectly permit any part to be copied or exposed, shall be regarded as violating one of the most solemn Obligations of the Order, and shall be disciplined accordingly.

The National Division direct, that the contents of the third page—" Our Emblem"—and the Odes and Responses used in the Ceremonies contained in this Blue Book, may be printed at the direction of Subordinate Divisions.

Subordinate Divisions may omit such portions of the Ritual as they think proper, except the forms for Examining Candidates, and administering the Obligations of the Order.

PUBLISHED BY

THE NATIONAL DIVISION OF NORTH AMERICA,

G. W. A. John Davies, Printer, 113 Nassau Street, New York.

1859.

REVISION OF THE RITUAL.

THE present revised edition of the Ritual of the Order of SONS OF TEMPERANCE of North America, was adopted by the National Division at its Fourteenth Annual Session, held in the City of Providence, State of Rhode Island, 1857.

OFFICERS OF THE NATIONAL DIVISION PRESENT.

M. D. McHENRY, *M. W. Patriarch.*
JAMES MACKEAN, *Acting M. W. Associate.*
FREDERICK A. FICKARDT, *M. W. Scribe.*
ROBERT M. FOUST, *M. W. Treasurer.*
CONVERS L. McCURDY, *Acting M. W. Chaplain.*
ANTHONY M. KENNEDY, *M. W. Conductor.*
ROBERT SALTER, *Acting M. W. Sentinel.*

REPRESENTATIVES OF GRAND DIVISIONS PRESENT.

EASTERN NEW YORK.
  James Mackean,
  Enoch Jacobs,
  Wm. H. Armstrong,
  Alex. Campbell,
  John Davies,
  H. S. Allen,
  Samuel Inslee.
WESTERN NEW YORK.
  G. W. Jermain,
  P. D. Walter.
NEW JERSEY.
  Silas L. Condict,
  P. Mason,
  P. F. Slack,
  W. W. Parkhurst.
MARYLAND.
  Benjamin E. Gantt.
PENNSYLVANIA.
  Robert M. Foust,
  J. C. Sims,
  J. H. Lewars,
  F. A. Fickardt.
CONNECTICUT.
  D. W. Lathrop.
MASSACHUSETTS.
  W. R. Stacy,
  W. H. Willson,
  H. D. Cushing,
  S. H. Hodges,
  F. A. Kingsbury,
  C. L. McCurdy.
VIRGINIA.
  Daniel Dodson,
  George A. Bruce.
MAINE.
  E. W. Jackson,
  Alvan Bolster,
  J. B. Thorndike,
  Sidney Perham.
OHIO.
  Samuel F. Cary,

INDIANA.
  Wm. H. Hannaman.
  J. W. Egelston,
  J. H. Batty.
TENNESSEE.
  Isaac Litton.
NORTH CAROLINA.
  Richard Stirling,
  C. P. Jones.
RHODE ISLAND.
  Philip B. Stiness,
  Silas Hemenway,
  G. R. Keymer,
  Daniel Wilkinson,
  Ira Cowee,
  T. W. Wood,
  Robert Allyn,
  Albert Holbrook,
  Albert Anthony.
MISSOURI.
  E. Wallingford.
NEW HAMPSHIRE.
  S. W. Buffum.
SOUTH CAROLINA.
  A. M. Kennedy,
  Nathaniel Tylee.
NEW BRUNSWICK.
  Robert Salter,
  James Olive,
  Richard Seely,
  John Frazer,
  Samuel Robinson.
IOWA.
  M. D. McHenry.
NOVA SCOTIA.
  Alex. McArthur,
  James Mosher.
VERMONT.
  Rennsalaer Tute,
  B. W. Burt,
  L. Sheldon.
CANADA EAST
  J. S Hall,
  George Mathison.

COMMITTEE OF REVISION.

FREDERICK A. FICKARDT,   EDWARD PAXSON,   JAMES MACKEAN.

The Ritual as revised and amended was unanimously agreed to.

OUR EMBLEM.

THE Star represents the light which TEMPERANCE has shed upon the world in darkness: a Pole Star to the wandering and tempest-tossed—a Morning Star to a brighter day—one of the brightest luminaries in the constellation of Virtues.

The Triangle, in allusion to the unalterable truth of mathematical and geometrical figures and quantities, is intended to represent the cardinal principles of the Order—LOVE, PURITY, and FIDELITY;—LOVE, the inspiring motive to do good to all men, and especially to the Brotherhood; PURITY in heart and conduct, and freedom from all base and selfish motives and views; and FIDELITY in redeeming every vow and pledge, and in promoting the interest of the Order in the world.

PASSWORDS.

I. All the general Passwords of the Order emanate from the Most Worthy Patriarch of the National Division of North America.

II. The general Passwords are :
1. An Annual Password for Grand Divisions.
2. A Quarterly Password and Explanation for Subordinate Divisions.
3. An Annual Traveling Password and Explanation for Subordinate Divisions, to be accompanied by the Traveling Card.

III. All Annual Passwords shall be changed at the first meeting in October.

IV. In changing the Quarterly Password and Explanation, the Worthy Patriarch shall direct the Financial Scribe to call the roll ; each Brother, as his name is called, will step up and receive it from the Worthy Patriarch, in a low whisper.

V. Brothers shall not be allowed to visit Divisions, other than those to which they are attached, without the Quarterly Password and its Explanation, and the Salutation ; or the Traveling Password and its Explanation, with the Card, and the Salutation ; unless vouched for by a Brother in good standing.

TRAVELING BROTHERS.

I. The Traveling Password and Explanation shall be given by the Worthy Patriarch to Brothers going abroad, who may be in regular standing at the time of making application for the same.

II. When a Brother wishes to visit by the Traveling Password, Explanation, and Card, he shall announce his name, the Division of which he is a member, and that he desires admittance by the Traveling Password and Explanation, to the outside Sentinel—the

Outside Sentinel shall announce it to the Inside Sentinel, who shall announce it to the Division. The Worthy Patriarch shall then direct him to be admitted to the Ante-room. The acting Past Worthy Patriarch retires, examines him in the Traveling Password and Explanation, in a whisper, and obtains his Card. If the P. W. P. is satisfied, he will re-enter, report the applicant correct in the Password and Explanation, and present the Card to the Worthy Patriarch, who, on finding the same correct, shall order the Brother to be admitted—observing, however, that he gives the Salutation.

III. A Traveling Brother may be admitted on the Traveling Password and Explanation in use at the date of his Card.

IV. It shall be proper for a Worthy Patriarch to communicate the Traveling Password and Explanation to a Past Worthy Patriarch.

GAVEL.

One Rap of the Gavel calls to order, and seats the Division.

Two Raps call up the Officers.

Three Raps call up the Division.

Four Raps call up the Division to form the Circle of Fraternity, and in Salute.

CUSTODY OF BLUE BOOKS.

The Blue Books and Cards should be kept by the Worthy Patriarch, who is responsible for them. They will be more carefully preserved by being kept in a suitable box.

If the Worthy Patriarch expects to be absent, he should place the box containing them in possession of the Worthy Associate, with the key.

The Worthy Patriarch may allow any Officer to take the Card containing his part, for the purpose of learning it—requiring it to be returned within a reasonable time.

After Initiation the Conductor should collect the Cards, and deliver them to the Worthy Patriarch.

REGALIA.

To preserve uniformity, all Subordinate Divisions of the Sons of Temperance shall be known by their Badge : White Collar, White Tassels, and Rosette of Red, White, and Blue, corresponding with the Motto, " Love, Purity, and Fidelity." To distinguish the Brothers filling the various stations, the following Emblems shall be added to their Badge :

Acting Past Worthy Patriarch—Flat Silver Star, six points, about three inches from point to point, on a ground of Red Velvet, circular form, trimmed with Silver Cord and Blue Ribbon, worn on left breast.

Worthy Patriarch—Cross Silver Mallets to correspond, same ground and trimmings, worn as above.

Worthy Associate—Miniature Collar, as above.

Recording Scribe—Cross Pens and Scroll, as above.

Assistant Recording Scribe—Single Pen, as above.

Financial Scribe—Cross Pens, as above.

Treasurer—Cross Keys, as above.

Chaplain—Open Book, as above.

Conductor—Cross Wands, as above.

Assistant Conductor—Goblet, as above.

Inside Sentinel—Cross Swords, as above.

Outside Sentinel—An Eye, as above.

Past' Worthy Patriarch, and Members of a Grand Division.— Red Collar, Rosette of Blue, White, and Red, Silver Button in the center, Silver Tassels, and Silver Lace half inch wide around the outside and inside edges.

Deputy Grand Worthy Patriarch—A gilt six-pointed Star and Triangle, suspended by a blue ribbon from Regalia, on left breast.

Past Grand Worthy Patriarchs and Members of the National Division—Blue Collar, Rosette of Red, Blue, and White, Gold Button in the center, Gold Lace and Tassels, in style corresponding with the above.

The Conductor, Assistant Conductor, Inside Sentinel, and Outside Sentinel, shall each be also distinguished by an appropriate wand or staff.

OPENING SERVICE.

[*Precisely at the appointed time, the W. P. should take the chair, and give one rap with the gavel.*

The Con., immediately on hearing the rap, shall stand up in his place and make proclamation as follows:]

Con. The Worthy Patriarch being now about to open —— Division No. —, in accordance with the established Usages of the Order of the Sons of Temperance, if there be any present not justly privileged to remain, they will please retire. The Officers and Brothers will clothe themselves in appropriate Regalia, and take their places.

W. P. The Brother Conductor will see if the Officers are at their appointed stations, and report.

[*The Con. will begin with the O. S. and examine each station up to the W. P., and report vacancies, if any.*

The W. P. shall fill vacancies, and the names of Brothers so appointed shall be entered on the minutes.]

[*One rap.*]

W. P. Let no Brother leave his place, unless directed, till after the Examination. The Assistant Conductor will now take charge of the outer door, and desire the Outside Sentinel to present himself for Examination. The Inside Sentinel will pass the Brother Assistant Conductor.

[*The O. S. enters.*]

O. S. I await your pleasure, Worthy Patriarch.

W. P. Your duty, Brother?

O. S. To guard well the outer door—admit no one without the Quarterly Password, unless directed by the Worthy Patriarch through the Inside Sentinel—and forewarn Brothers not to disturb the Opening, Initiatory, or Closing Ceremonies.

W. P. You will now advance and give the Password. (*Does sp.*) Right, Brother—your station requires, and we expect it will receive your strict attention. The Inside Sentinel will pass the Brother to his post.

[*The O. S. and A. C. resume their stations.*]

W. P. The Conductor and Assistant Conductor will now advance and give the Explanation to the Quarterly Password.

[*They do so, in a whisper.*]

W. P. Correct, Brothers. Your next duty?

Con. To satisfy ourselves that all present are equally qualified—and if any give more or less than this, to report to you.

W. P. You will now carefully perform that duty.

[*The Con. shall take the right, and the A. C. the left, of the W. P., and carefully examine every one present. If any give more or less than the Explanation, the Con., or A. C., shall report the name, and Division, of the Brother incorrect.*]

W. P. Can any Brother vouch that this gentleman is a Member of our Order in regular standing?

[*If there be no voucher, the person must retire, unless he give the W. P., or P. W. P., the Traveling Password, Explanation, and Card—in which case he shall be permitted to remain.*]

Con. Worthy Patriarch—All correct on the right.

A. C. Worthy Patriarch—All correct on the left.

W. P. The Inside Sentinel will now rehearse his duty.

I. S. To allow none to enter or retire during the Opening, Initiatory, or Closing Ceremonies—to admit no one at any time without the Entering Signal, and the Explanation to the Quarterly Password, unless by your direction.

W. P. An important duty, Brother—faithfully perform it.

[*Three raps. W. P. rises.*]

W. P. OFFICERS AND BROTHERS:

We meet to interchange the greetings of an exalted friendship; to counsel, admonish, and strengthen one another in the discharge of duty; and to deliberate on the means best adapted to promote the objects for which we are associated.

It is but reasonable to expect that matters will be introduced which will strike your minds in different forms. To discuss such matters with freedom, is our equal privilege, and to yield a cheerful compliance to the constituted majority, is our equal duty. In this an opportunity is afforded to manifest our love for the Order, by guarding against every ungenerous sentiment or dishonorable action.

Our mission is one of benevolence—to destroy the destroyer of millions—to conquer the enemy of our people, and promote the virtue and happiness of mankind.

Let us, therefore, be strong and temperate in our cause—prompt in the transaction of business—courteous in debate, (ever keeping in mind that he who is slow to anger is better than the mighty, and he that ruleth his own spirit than he that taketh a city), careful to avoid all wrangling and vain dispute, charitable in our judgment of others, and faithful to our vows.

Thus shall we most surely advance the interests of our Order, and illustrate how sweet and pleasant it is for Brothers to dwell together in unity.

[*Division sing:*]

> Yes, we in those principles join,
>   And such shall our actions display ;
> Our hands and our hearts shall combine
>   To extend their beneficent sway.

> Our laws we will ever respect,
>   Arise all contention above—
> And stand by each other erect,
>   In Purity, Friendship, and Love.

[*One rap.*]

[*Prayer by the Chaplain, or reading of the Scriptures.*]

W. P. I now declare this Division open for the transaction of its appropriate business, and the propagation of the principles of Temperance, Benevolence, and Brotherly Love.

W. P. The Recording Scribe will now read the Minutes.

[*Proceed after this according to the Order of Business.*]

NOTE.—No Retiring Password is to be used. The W. P. may, under important circumstances, direct the Inside Sentinel to permit no Member to leave the Room.

ORDER OF BUSINESS

1. Opening Division.
2. Roll of Officers called.
3. Services of Chaplain.
4. Reading Minutes.
5. Dues and other Moneys collected.
6. Reception of Communications.
7. Reports of Investigating Committees.
8. Balloting for Candidates.
9. Initiation of Candidates.
10. Are any of the Brothers sick?
11. Has any Brother violated his Pledge?
12. Has any Brother a friend to propose as a proper person to become a Son of Temperance?
13. What have you done during the past week to advance the interests of the Order, and save your fellow-men from the evils of Intemperance?
14. Reports of Visiting Committees.
15. Reports of Standing Committees.
16. Reports of Special Committees.
17. Election of Officers.
18. New Business.
19. Has any Brother anything to offer for the good of the Division?
20. Adjournment.

CEREMONY OF INITIATION.

[*One rap.*]

W. P. The Brother Assistant Conductor will see if there are any Candidates to be initiated.

[*If any—*]

A. C. Worthy Patriarch, Mr. ———— is in waiting.

W. P. You will now conduct our Worthy Associate to make the necessary examination. The Brother who proposed the Candidate, will retire and introduce him to the Worthy Associate and Assistant Conductor.

[*If the Brother who proposed him should not be present, any other Brother who can vouch for the Candidate may perform the introduction.*

After the introduction the Brother may return to the Division.

While the examination is going on in the Ante-room, the Con. should see that the Members are arranged to the best advantage, and that the Water, Goblets, Regalia, etc., are in readiness, so that nothing shall occur to mar the Ceremony.]

W. A. SIR:—You are at the threshold of an Institution, whose central principle is Total Abstinence from all Intoxicating Drinks, and whose prominent characteristic is a self-denying devotion to the good of Mankind.

On entering our Order, you will be required to take a solemn Obligation to abstain from the manufacture, traffic, and use, as a beverage, of all Spirituous and Malt Liquors, Wine, and Cider.

Your religious and political opinions we leave with your conscience and your country. As a protection from idle curiosity, and the intrusion of unsuitable persons, certain Rites have been established, which will neither harm your person nor offend your self-respect—and we assure you that there is no shield thrown over the guilty, no snare laid for the innocent.

With this understanding, is it your desire to become a Member of our Order?

[*The Candidate, if willing, replies :* It is.]

W. A. What is your age?

*Are you exempt from disease of a serious nature?

[*Candidate replies.*

At any point in the Examination the Candidate may re-tire, or be rejected if disqualified, and the W. A. will report accordingly. In either case, the Initiation Fee, if paid, shall be refunded.]

W. A. Please be seated until I report to my Brothers.

[*The A. C. remains with the Candidate. The W. A. re-enters the Division.*]

W. A. Worthy Patriarch—I have examined the Candidate, and find him qualified and willing to proceed.

---

* This question is to be asked only in the case of beneficiaries.

W. P. Let every Brother keep his place, and observe the utmost decorum during the Ceremony of Initiation.

[*Perfect order prevails.*]

W. P. Let the Signal be given.

[*The I. S. gives* ONE *knock on the door. The A. C. hearing the Signal, leads the Candidate to the door, and directs him to give* TWO *knocks.*]

I. S. Who knocks?

A. C. A stranger.

I. S. Why cometh the stranger?

A. C. To enter the gates of our Order.

I. S. Is he worthy?

A. C. He has so been found.

I. S. Our doors are only closed to the unworthy.

[*The door is thrown open—the Con. receives the Candidate by the hand.*]

Con. Welcome to the worthy!

[*Three raps. Division sing:*]

> Traveler through a world of danger,
> Welcome to a refuge here;
> Safety to the trusting stranger,
> Safety from the tempter's snare.

[*During the singing the Candidate is led around the room, the Con. on his left, and A. C. on his right—(if there are several Candidates, it is best to walk single file, the Con.*

in front, A. C. behind). When the singing is finished, the Con. and Candidate, and A. C., should be about the center of the room, facing the Chaplain.]

[*One rap.*]

Chap.* Who hath woe ?   Who hath sorrow ?
.   Who hath contentions ?
    Who hath wounds without cause ?

P. W. P. They that tarry long at the wine !
    They that seek strong drink !

Chap. Look not upon the wine when it is red,
    When it giveth its color in the cup—
    For at the last it biteth like a serpent,
    And stingeth like an adder.

Div. respond. Look not upon the wine !

A. C. Behold another
    Who renounces the wine,
    And turns away from strong drink !

Div. respond. Welcome !   Welcome !

Con. Yes, welcome !
    Here, you are safe
    From the all-pervading Destroyer !
    He comes in the mask of kindness—
    He whispers, " Be merry, be social,"
    And proffers the cup of enchantment.

---

* Divisions having no Chaplain may assign this part to any suitable Brother.

17

Div. respond. Dash it down!

Con. Yes, dash it down!
Touch but a drop with your lips,
And behold a vast ocean surrounds you,
To whelm and sink you forever!
Trust not the perfidious Destroyer—
Wherever he cometh, he smiteth!
He spares not the high nor the humble;
He withers the vigor of youth,
And dishonors the gray hairs of age!

A. C. *One* circle he never can enter—
One place is secure from his ravage—
That glorious refuge is *here!*

Div. respond. It is here! It is here!

Con. Then, welcome again to the stranger,
Who heeds not the voice of the Tempter—
But turns from the snares that beset him,
To enter this Circle of Honor—
Where *each* is a shield to the *other*,
And *all* to the world an *example!*

I will now introduce you to our Worthy Patriarch.

[*Three raps. Division sing.*]

Blest be the tie that binds
Our hearts in purest love.
The fellowship of kindred minds
Is like to that above.

[*During the singing the Candidate is conducted around the room, to the front of the W. P.*]

2

Con. Worthy Patriarch, I have the pleasure of introduc-ing Mr. —— ——, who has been duly proposed and accepted as a suitable Candidate for Initiation into our Order.

W. P. Every Brother will place his right hand on the left breast, and the Candidate will do the same, as a token of Fidelity.

RESPECTED SIR:—You are about to take upon yourself an important and solemn Obligation, which, as you have been informed, will not interfere with your religious or political opinions.

Do you, without reserve, solemnly pledge your honor, in the presence of these Witnesses, that you will neither *make*, *buy*, *sell*, *nor use*, *as a beverage*, *any Spirituous or Malt Liquors*, *Wine*, *or Cider?*

Do you furthermore pledge yourself faithfully to observe the Constitution and By-Laws of this Division, and the Rules and Usages of the Order; and never to divulge any Password, Ceremony, or other Private Matter of the Order, except to those legally authorized to receive them—and whether your connection with the Order shall continue or not, to consider your Obligation in this respect binding to the end of life?

Do you furthermore pledge yourself to promote the har-mony, advance the interest, and preserve unsullied, on your part, the reputation of the Sons of Temperance?

Do you thus solemnly promise? If so, answer, I do.

[*Candidate replies. After the Obligation the Brothers drop their hands.*]

[*The W. A. steps down, and the Con. pours water into a glass goblet for the Candidate (if more than one Candidate, a goblet for each), and in another for the W. P., during which the W. A., pointing to the water, addresses the Candidate.*]

W. A. This which you now behold is sparkling water—
The beverage prepared by God himself,
To nourish and invigorate his creatures,
And beautify his footstool.
As thus you see its countless drops unite
And blend in one, so may we blend together
In one unruffled stream,
Whose purity shall wash away the stains
Of black Intemperance.

[*The W. A. resumes his place. The Con. hands a goblet of water to the W. P. and another to the Candidate.*]

W. P. And as one stain would discolor this whole element of purity, so would one unworthy Member bring reproach upon our whole Order. (*Addressing the Division.*) Bearing this in mind, let us be faithful to our Obligations.

[*Each Brother places his right hand on the left breast, and says: I will.*]

W. P. (*Addressing the Candidate.*) In this pure element, then, an emblem of our Order, we solemnly pledge Fidelity to each other.

[*W. P. and Candidate drink.*]

Chap. May the blessing of Heaven rest upon our Brother, and upon our Order forever.

[*Division sing :*]

Father of mercies ! condescend
To hear our fervent prayer,
While now our Brother we commend
To thy paternal care.

[*The W. P. steps forward.*]

W. P.* Confiding in your integrity, I now invest you with this badge, and proclaim you a SON OF TEMPERANCE! Wear it, Brother, as an emblem of Virtue—wear it proudly! In the name of this great Brotherhood, I charge you, defend it! By the recollection of the past, the dignity of the present, and the solemnity of the future, I invoke you to guard it from dishonor ! [*W. P. resumes his place.*]

[*The W. A. steps forward.*]

W. A. Hail, Son of Temperance!
And be that name thy glory and thy shield.
High now is thy position
Among the sons of men—
Responsible and great
The duties it involves.
The foes of Temperance, and the friends alike,
Will look to your example,
And judge the cause by you:
Be faithful to the cause, the cause of all mankind.
Be faithful to *yourself*,
For all our laws require,
Tend to *your* lasting good.

[*One rap.*]

---

* Where Lady Visitors are admitted, the Worthy Patriarch may appoint one of them to perform this part.

[The Con. leads the Initiate to the P. W. P.]

Con. Past Worthy Patriarch—I here present Brother
—— ——, who having been obligated and invested with
the badge of our Order, is respectfully referred to you for
further instruction.

[The P. W. P. rises.]

P. W. P. BROTHER:—From a favorable opinion enter-
tained of you by the Members of this Division, you have
been admitted to the privileges of our Order. It is a mark
of our esteem and confidence, that we thus extend to you a
Brother's hand and a Brother's welcome!

You will be expected to attend regularly our stated meet-
ings; and are bound to observe our Laws and Usages by the
strongest of human ties—YOUR SACRED HONOR.

In the Division let your conduct exhibit a manly
frankness and brotherly courtesy. Above all, be careful to
cultivate a forgiving spirit. Write the errors of your
Brothers in sand; but engrave their virtues on the tablets
of enduring memory, that you may learn to imitate them.

In defense of our principles, remember that unwavering
Fidelity is a better advocate than violent denunciation. No
imprudence should excite a suspicion of your constancy.
Associate with the votaries of folly only to reform them.

Let no consideration of personal regard mislead you into
recommending an unsuitable person. Neither the wealth
of an individual—his influential position in society—nor the
most commanding talents—can entitle him to approach our
Circle, if, with all these, he is wanting in integrity; but the
upright, honest man, however humble his position, shall be

welcome; for integrity with us is of more price than silver and gold.

Finally, Brother, ever bear in mind the Motto character-istic of our Order, as portrayed in the colors of the Badge—the Red, the White, the Blue—expressive of LOVE, PURITY, and FIDELITY:—LOVE for your Brothers in sickness and in health; PURITY of heart and life; and FIDELITY to the solemn and binding Obligation you have this night voluntarily taken upon yourself.

And may the GREAT PATRIARCH above direct us to that haven of rest where Sorrow is never known, and where Love and Harmony shall reign forever!

[*Three raps.   Division sing:*]

Spirit of Love ! benign and mild—
    Inspire our hearts—our souls possess ;
Repel each passion rude and wild—
    And bless us, as we aim to bless.

[*One rap.*]

[*During the singing the Con. leads the newly initiated Brother to the center of the room, facing the Chaplain, who rises and says:*]

Chap.   BROTHER:—Of all things, Wisdom is profitable to man. The fear of the Lord is the beginning of Wisdom. Tribulation and anguish shall come upon every son of man that doeth evil; but glory, and honor, and peace to him that worketh good.

Go not in the way of evil men, for it is as darkness; they eat the bread of wickedness, and drink the wine of violence; but the way of the just is as the shining light that shineth more and more unto the perfect day. Therefore, be not overcome of evil, but overcome evil with good. If thine enemy hunger, feed him—if he thirst, give him drink.

There is no vice which, in one black and awful gulf, swallows up so much of hope and happiness as Intemperance. It prostrates all that is great, and blights all that is good, in humanity. The man of honor it betrays into infamy—the man of virtue into sin. It touches the manly frame, and it is clothed with corruption. It seizes the intellect, and its divine lineaments are blotted out forever. It breathes upon the holy affections, and they are blasted. It destroys the tenderest ties of social life, exiles the sweet endearments of home, and robs the earth of its loveliness.

Your name is enrolled among the champions of Temperance. Her cause is to be your cause, her honor is confided to your keeping, and your rewards are to be gathered from her triumphs. "In her right hand is length of days; in her left hand, riches and honor."

She touches with her magic wand the delicate framework of the human body, and it is clothed with new vigor and beauty. She sheds her mild radiance over the intellect, and its light and glory beam forth with increasing brightness. She breathes upon man's social nature, and it blooms with a fresher and more charming fragrance. She receives under her holy guardianship the loveliness of woman and the innocence of childhood, and they are protected from a sea of evils. At her approach the fountain of domestic affection sends forth its streams more joyously, spreading the music of rippling waters among the green vales of home.

The light of a pure life is a beacon star of salvation—but a base example leads to death. Therefore, I charge you to do nothing whereby a Brother is made weak, or stumbleth.

In conclusion, Brother, remember that life is brief. Whatever your hand finds to do for the good of man, do quickly; for the night cometh when no man can work.

May your course be full of joy to others—and when your own star shall set at life's close, may it set as sets the Morning Star, which goeth not down behind the darkened West, but melts away into the brightness of heaven!

[*Four raps.*]

[*The Officers* (except the Sentinels and Con.), *Brothers, and Lady Visitors, form the Circle of Fraternity around the Con. and Brother, as follows:*

during which the Division sing?]

Once more we here the Pledge renew
Of strict FIDELITY;
Still to our maxims ever true,
To LOVE and PURITY.

No unkind words our lips shall pass,
No envy sour the mind;
But each shall seek the common weal,
The good of all mankind.

[*At the close of the singing the W. P. steps into the Circle.*]

W. P. BROTHER :—While we rejoice at our own deliverance, let us remember that the world has claims upon us. Intemperance is peculiarly a social evil. We therefore resist its terrible power by a social and fraternal combination. We join hand in hand, and heart to heart, in this Institution, to protect ourselves and meet a common foe with the victorious power of Combination.

In the Brothers here assembled, you behold a type of our mission's fulfillment. This is a sober world in miniature—and we seek to enlarge this circle of sobriety, until it shall embrace the entire Brotherhood of Man. Our Order is sight to the blind, strength to the weak, a shield to the innocent, and a comfort, and blessing, and hope to all.

Relying, therefore, upon the greatness and justice of our Cause, and the purity of our motives, we must move steadily forward until our purposes are accomplished.

In conclusion, Brother (*taking him by the hand*), I congratulate you most cordially on your accession to our Fraternity, and, with the best wishes for your prosperity, I commend you to their friendship. (*Turning to the Division.*) Brothers, receive your Brother.

[*After an appropriate period of congratulation, during which the Con. remains with the Brother, the W. P. calls the Division to order.*]

W. P. The newly initiated Brother will please step for·
ward. The Conductor will attend him.

[*Con. and Brother step forward.*]

W. P. BROTHER :—I now give you the Password for the
current Quarter (*gives in a whisper*). This Password is given
to the Outside Sentinel, who will permit you to pass. You
then advance to the inner door, and give one rap, which is
the Entering Signal ; the Inside Sentinel presents himself, to
whom you give the Explanation, which I now give you
(*gives in a whisper*). This Explanation will admit you to
the Division. After you have entered, advance to the front
of the Past Worthy Patriarch, and salute him thus, (*right
hand on the left breast*), he will acknowledge it by a slight
bow of the head, after which you will take your seat.

Should you wish to retire while the Division is in session,
you will salute the Past Worthy Patriarch in the same man·
ner as when you entered.

The Password, with its Explanation, and the Entering
Signal and the Salutation, will insure your welcome, during
the present Quarter, to any Subordinate Division of our
Order. A new Password and Explanation are given Quar·
terly. These words and Salutation are never to be given
out of a Division. This, Brother, is to prevent imposition.

And here I will remind you, that you are not to speak of
the private affairs of our Order, nor mention aught that is
spoken in the confidence of the Division Room, in the
presence of those who are not Members, for they are under
the sacred seal of your honor.

You will now sign our Constitution, after which the
Conductor will lead you to a seat.

CLOSING SERVICE.

W. P. Brother Financial Scribe, I will thank you to name the receipts of the evening.

[*The F. S. announces the receipts, which the R. S. enters on the Minutes.*]

[*Three raps.*]

W. P. OFFICERS AND BROTHERS :

I thank you for your attention this evening, and bespeak your continued presence as the best safeguard of your own happiness, the interests of the Division, and the vows of those who look to you for an example.

The business we have transacted, and the sympathies and resolves we have cherished, will contribute, I trust, to our individual and mutual advantage, and to the prosperity of our noble Order.

Let us retire with kindly feelings toward each other.

Remember the Pledge, be faithful to your duties, and zealous in doing good.

We will now sing No. — of our Closing Odes.

1.—CLOSING ODE.

A goodly thing it is to meet
In Friendship's circle bright,
Where nothing stains the pleasure sweet,
Nor dims the radiant light.

No happier meeting earth can see
Than where the joy we prove,
Of Temperance and Purity,
Fidelity and Love.

———•—•———

2.—CLOSING ODE.

Good night, good night to every one;
Be each heart free from care;
Let every Brother seek his home,
And find contentment there.

May joy beam with to-morrow's sun,
And every prospect shine;
While wife and friends laugh merrily
Without the aid of Wine.

W P   I now declare this Division closed.

[One rap.]

INSTALLATION SERVICE.

[*The Installation Service should be performed by the Grand Worthy Patriarch and Grand Conductor, or a Deputy Grand Worthy Patriarch, and a Deputy Grand Conductor. If this can not be done, let the Senior Past Worthy Patriarch of the Division present officiate as Deputy Grand Worthy Patriarch, appointing a Deputy Grand Conductor.*

The Installing Patriarch shall have power to decide objections, subject to the approval of the Grand Division; or, if he prefer, may allow the Officers of the previous Quarter to hold over until a decision shall be made.

The Installation Service may be performed publicly, but the Salutation must then be omitted.]

[*At the appointed time the G. C. will approach the inner door, and after giving the Entering Signal and Explanation, announce himself (as G. C.) to the I. S. The I. S. shall report to the W. P., who will direct his admission. On entering, the G. C. salutes the P. W. P. in the usual form, after which he will address the W. P.*]

G. C. Worthy Patriarch, the Grand Worthy Patriarch (*or Deputy G. W. P.*) is prepared to Install the Officers of this Division ; are you ready to receive him?

W. P. We are, Grand Conductor.

[*The G. C. retires, after giving the usual Salutation to the P. W. P.*

The G. W. P. and G. C. will approach the door and give the Entering Signal and announce themselves to the I. S.]

I. S. Worthy Patriarch, the Grand Worthy Patriarch and Grand Conductor are in waiting.

W. P. The Inside Sentinel will admit them.

[*Four raps.*]

[*As they enter the W. P. will give* FOUR *raps. The Division rises, and the G. W. P. and G. C. advance to the center of the room and salute the W. P., who, together with all the Brothers, return the Salutation. The following verse will be sung while the G. C. escorts the G. W. P. to the W. P.'s chair; the W. P. taking station on his right. The G. C. takes the Con's seat.*]

[*Division sing:*]*

> Thrice welcome, Brother, here we meet,
>> In Friendship's close communion join'd;
> Ye Sons of Temp'rance loud repeat
>> Your triumphs with one heart and mind.
> No angry passions here should mar
>> Our peace, or move our social band,
> For Friendship is our beacon star,
>> Our motto, "Union, Hand-in-hand."

[*One rap.*]

G. C. (*Rising.*) BROTHERS :—According to usage, we meet you here this evening to Install your Officers. Have they been constitutionally elected?

---

* The singing *may* be omitted when the Installation is performed by a Deputy.

Div. respond. They have.

G. C. The Recording Scribe will please announce them.

[*The R. S. announces the names of the Brothers, and the Offices to which they have been elected.*]

G. C. (*Addressing the W. P.*)* Has the Worthy Patriarch elect rendered that service to the Division which our Constitution requires, to render him eligible to that station?

W. P. He has.

G. C. If any Brother is aware of just reason why this Brother should not be inducted into the Office assigned to him, he now has an opportunity to announce it. (*If no reply.*) Then do I proclaim him eligible for Installation.

[*The G. W. P. appoints two Brothers to act as O. S. and I. S.*]

G. W. P. The Officers will now vacate their stations in order, and deliver up their books, implements, and badges of Office.

[*The W. P. delivers the Charter, Blue Books, and other documents in his possession, and lastly his badge, to the G. W. P.*]

G. W. P. The Grand Conductor will escort the Past Worthy Patriarch to his station.

---

* In a new Division omit this. Other alterations may also be necessary.

[The G. C. does so, and then returns. The W. A. then delivers to G. C. his badge—the R. S. his books and badge— the A. R. S. his badge—the F. S. his books and badge—the Treas. his books and badge—the Con. his staff and badge— the A. C. his staff and badge—the I. S. his staff and badge —and the O. S. his staff and badge.]

G. W. P. The Officers elect will now divest themselves of Regalia, and, in company with the Grand Conductor, retire to the ante-room. The Inside Sentinel will allow them to pass.

[They retire. The G. C. arranges them as follows : W. P., and W. A. on his left.—R. S. and A. R. S.—F. S. and Treas.—Con. and A. C.—I. S. and O. S.—arm in arm. When ready, the G. C. directs the I. S. to announce it. The G. W. P. orders them to be admitted.

As they enter, call up and sing the following verse—during which the G. C., with Officers elect, walk around the room ; at the close of the singing let it be so managed that they will be in front of seats on the right and left, so that they may be seated when called down.]

[Three raps.   Division sing :]

Whatever station we may fill
    In this exalted band,
Our plighted duties we shall still
    Achieve, with heart and hand ;
And evermore, through good and ill,
    By one another stand—
Whatever station we may fill
    In this exalted band.

[One rap.]

OUTSIDE SENTINEL.

G. W. P. The Grand Conductor will now present the Outside Sentinel elect to the Past Worthy Patriarch, and desire him to administer the Obligation of his Office.

G. C. Past Worthy Patriarch, I am directed by the Grand Worthy Patriarch to present Brother —— ——, Outside Sentinel elect of this Division, and request you to administer the Obligation of his Office.

P. W. P. Brother, you will place your right hand on the left breast. (*Does so.*)

You solemnly and unreservedly pledge your honor as a man, and as a Son of Temperance, to guard faithfully the outer door—admit no one without the Quarterly Password, unless by permission of the Worthy Patriarch, communicated through the Inside Sentinel—and perform all other duties belonging to the office of Outside Sentinel during the term of your election?

O. S. I do.

[*G. C. leads him to the G. W. P.*]

G. C. Grand Worthy Patriarch, the Brother has been obligated.

G. W. P. I now invest you with the badge of Office, and proclaim you Outside Sentinel of —— Division, No. —, for the present term. Receive your staff of Office. (*G. C. presents it.*) The faithful Sentinel is always a valiant soldier; be as active in promoting our glorious cause, as you are watchful in guarding the Division from intrusion. (*Resumes his chair.*)

G. C. Before you take your station, it is necessary to see that you are properly instructed in the Password. You will please give it to the Grand Worthy Patriarch.

[*O. S. gives the Password.*]

G. W. P. The Grand Conductor will escort the Brother to his station.

INSIDE SENTINEL.

G. W. P. The Grand Conductor will now present the Inside Sentinel elect to the Past Worthy Patriarch, and desire him to administer the Obligation of his Office.

G. C. Past Worthy Patriarch, I am directed by the Grand Worthy Patriarch to present Brother —— ———, Inside Sentinel elect of this Division, and request you to administer the Obligation of his Office.

P. W. P. Brother, you will place your right hand on the left breast. (*Does so*)

You solemnly and unreservedly pledge your honor as a man, and as a Son of Temperance, to guard the inner door of this Division—to allow no one to enter or retire during the Opening, Initiatory, or Closing Ceremonies —to admit no one at any time without the Entering Signal, and the Explanation to the Quarterly Password, nor allow any to retire without giving the Salutation, unless directed so to do by the Worthy Patriarch— and faithfully to perform all other duties belonging to the Office of Inside Sentinel during the term of your election?

I. S. I do.

[*The G. C. leads him to the G. W. P.*]

G. C. Grand Worthy Patriarch, the Brother has been obligated.

G. W. P. I now invest you with the badge of Office, and proclaim you Inside Sentinel of —— Division, No. —, for the present term. Receive your staff of Office. (*G. C. presents it.*) Vigilant at your post, be equally vigilant in your conduct.

You will please give me the Explanation of the Password.

[*I. S. gives the Explanation.*]

G. W. P. The Grand Conductor will escort the Brother to his station.

ASSISTANT CONDUCTOR.

G. W. P. The Grand Conductor will now present the Assistant Conductor elect to the Past Worthy Patriarch, and desire him to administer the Obligation of his Office.

G. C. Past Worthy Patriarch, I am directed by the Grand Worthy Patriarch to present Brother —— ——, Assistant Conductor elect of this Division, and request you to administer the Obligation of his Office.

P. W. P. Brother, you will place your right hand on your left breast. (*Does so.*)

You solemnly and unreservedly pledge your honor as a man, and as a Son of Temperance, to render timely assist-

ance to the Conductor in the discharge of his duties—
to carefully examine all on the left at the opening of
the Division, and report those incorrect to the Worthy
Patriarch—that you will never expose, or cause to be
exposed, to any person not a Member of our Order, any
part of the Ceremonies to you intrusted—that you will
not keep a copy of them, nor allow any other person so
to do—that you will promptly deliver them up to the
Worthy Patriarch, when called upon so to do—and that
you will faithfully perform all other duties belonging to
the office of Assistant Conductor during the term of
your election ?

A. C.   I do.

[*G. C. leads him to the G. W. P.*]

G. C.   Grand Worthy Patriarch, the Brother has been
obligated.

G. W. P.   I now invest you with the badge of Office, and
proclaim you Assistant Conductor of —— Division, No —,
for the present term.   Receive your staff of Office—(*G. C.
presents it*).   Always keep the radiant Star of our Order in
view, that those who follow your steps may be led within
the influence of its benignant beams.

The Grand Conductor will escort the Brother to his
station.

CONDUCTOR.

G. W. P.   The Grand Conductor will now present the
Conductor elect to the Past Worthy Patriarch, and desire
him to administer the Obligation of his Office.

G. C. Past Worthy Patriarch, I am directed by the Grand Worthy Patriarch to present Brother —— ———, Conductor elect of this Division, and request you to administer the Obligation of his Office.

P. W. P. Brother, you will place your right hand on the left breast. (*Does so.*)

You solemnly and unreservedly pledge your honor as a man, and as a Son of Temperance, to examine with circumspection every person on the right at the opening of the Division, and report any incorrect to the Worthy Patriarch—that you will never expose, or cause to be exposed, to any person not a Member of our Order, any part of the Ceremonies to you intrusted— that you will not keep a copy of them, nor allow any other person so to do—that you will promptly deliver them up to the Worthy Patriarch when called upon so to do—and that you will faithfully perform all other duties belonging to the Office of Conductor during the term of your election?

Con. I do.

[*G. C. leads him to the G. W. P.*]

G. C. Grand Worthy Patriarch, the Brother has been obligated.

G. W. P. I now invest you with the badge of Office, and proclaim you Conductor of —— Division, No. —, for the present term. Receive your staff of Office—(*G. C. presents it*). Let your demeanor be such that you may always be considered a trustworthy guide; not only here, but through the paths of life.

The Grand Conductor will escort the Brother to his station.

TREASURER.

G. W. P. The Grand Conductor will now present the Treasurer elect to the Past Worthy Patriarch, and desire him to administer the Obligation of his Office.

G. C. Past Worthy Patriarch, I am directed by the Grand Worthy Patriarch to present Brother —— ———, Treasurer elect of this Division, and request you to administer the Obligation of his Office.

P. W. P. Brother, you will place your right hand on the left breast. (*Does so.*)

You solemnly and unreservedly pledge your honor as a man, and as a Son of Temperance, to hold in trust all moneys of this Division, until the expiration of your term, unless otherwise ordered by the Division—to pay promptly therefrom all orders drawn by the Worthy Patriarch, attested by the Recording Scribe—to keep a full and correct account of all moneys received and expended—give the Division a monthly statement of the funds—deliver up to your successor in Office, or any other person duly authorized to receive them, at the close of your term, or earlier if called upon so to do, all moneys, books, papers, and other property of the Division in your possession or under your control—and to perform such other duties as Treasurer, as the Constitution, By-Laws, and Regulations of this Division require?

Treas. I do.

[*G. C. leads him to the G. W. P.*]

G. C. Grand Worthy Patriarch, the Brother has been obligated.

G. W. P. I now invest you with the badge of Office, and proclaim you Treasurer of —— Division, No. —, for the present term. Receive the books and documents belonging to your Office—(*they are presented*). In confiding to you the treasure of the Division, your Brothers confide in the treasure of your honor. Let *their* confidence be fully justified by *your* integrity.

The Grand Conductor will escort the Brother to his station.

FINANCIAL SCRIBE.

G. W. P. The Grand Conductor will now present the Financial Scribe elect to the Past Worthy Patriarch, and desire him to administer the Obligation of his Office.

G. C. Past Worthy Patriarch, I am directed by the Grand Worthy Patriarch to present Brother —— ——, Financial Scribe elect of this Division, and request you to administer the Obligation of his Office.

P. W. P. Brother, you will place your right hand on the left breast. (*Does so.*)

You solemnly and unreservedly pledge your honor as a man, and as a Son of Temperance, to keep just and true accounts between this Division and its Members—credit the amounts paid, and pay the same over to the Treasurer immediately—perform faithfully and promptly, to the utmost of your ability, all other duties belonging to the Office of Financial Scribe—and deliver up at the expiration of your term, all books, papers, and other documents belonging to the Division in your possession?

F. S.   I do.

[*G. C. leads him to the G. W. P.*]

G. C.   Grand Worthy Patriarch, the Brother has been obligated.

G. W. P.   I now invest you with the badge of Office, and proclaim you Financial Scribe of —— Division, No. —, for the present term.   You will now receive the books and documents belonging to your Office—(*they are presented*). It is the peculiar privilege of your station to illustrate most conspicuously our cardinal principle, FIDELITY.   Let it be the motto of your conduct, and the ornament of your life.

The Grand Conductor will escort the Brother to his station.

ASSISTANT RECORDING SCRIBE.

G. W. P.   The Grand Conductor will now present the Assistant Recording Scribe elect to the Past Worthy Patriarch, and desire him to administer the Obligation of his Office.

G. C.   Past Worthy Patriarch, I am directed by the Grand Worthy Patriarch to present Brother —— ——, Assistant Recording Scribe elect of this Division, and request you to administer the Obligation of his Office.

P. W. P. Brother, you will place your right hand on the left breast. (*Does so.*)

You solemnly and unreservedly pledge your honor as a man, and as a Son of Temperance, to render such proper and timely aid to the Recording Scribe in the performance of his duties, as he or the Division may require of you ?

A. R. S. I do.

[*G. C. leads him to the G. W. P.*]

G. C. Grand Worthy Patriarch, the Brother has been obligated.

G. W. P. I now invest you with the badge of Office, and proclaim you Assistant Recording Scribe of —— Division, No. —, for the present term. Your Office requires an attentive ear, a prompt and ready hand. Be constant in season and out of season.

The Grand Conductor will escort the Brother to his station.

RECORDING SCRIBE.

G. W. P. The Grand Conductor will now present the Recording Scribe elect to the Past Worthy Patriarch, and desire him to administer the Obligation of his Office.

G. C. Past Worthy Patriarch, I am directed by the Grand Worthy Patriarch to present Brother —— ——, Recording Scribe elect of this Division, and request you to administer the Obligation of his Office.

P. W. P. Brother, you will place your right hand on the left breast. (*Does so.*)

> You solemnly and unreservedly pledge your honor as a man, and as a Son of Temperance, to keep a fair and impartial record of the proceedings of this Division—notify all Subordinate Divisions, not more than ten miles from this place, within four weeks after, of the name, occupation, and residence of every person suspended, rejected, or expelled from this Division—make out at the end of your term, for the Division, a full report of the proceedings during your term, and also the Quarterly Returns for the Grand Division—perform all other duties belonging to the Office of Recording Scribe—and deliver up at the expiration of your term, all books, papers, or other property in your possession belonging to your Office?

R. S. I do.

[*G. C. leads him to the G. W. P.*]

G. C. Grand Worthy Patriarch, the Brother has been obligated.

G. W. P. I now invest you with the badge of Office, and proclaim you Recording Scribe of —— Division, No. —, for the present term. You will now receive the books and documents belonging to your Office—(*they are presented*). Be diligent, faithful, and impartial—that your reputation may remain, like your record, without blot or blemish.

The Grand Conductor will escort the Brother to his station.

WORTHY ASSOCIATE.

G. W. P. The Grand Conductor will now present the Worthy Associate elect to the Past Worthy Patriarch, and desire him to administer the Obligation of his Office.

C. C. Past Worthy Patriarch, I am directed by the Grand Worthy Patriarch to present Brother —— ———, Worthy Associate elect of this Division, and request you to administer the Obligation of his Office.

P. W. P. You will place your right hand on the left breast. (*Does so.*)

You solemnly and unreservedly pledge your honor as a man, and as a Son of Temperance, to counsel and support the Worthy Patriarch in the discharge of his duties, and in his absence officiate in his place—that you will never expose, or cause to be exposed, to any person not a Member of our Order, the Ceremonies intrusted to your care, nor any part thereof—that you will not keep a copy of them, nor allow any person so to do—that you will promptly deliver them up when requested by the Worthy Patriarch, or his Deputy— and that you will perform all other duties belonging to the Office of Worthy Associate, to the best of your judgment and ability, during the term of your election ?

W. A. I do.

(*G. C. leads him to the G. W. P.*)

G. C. Grand Worthy Patriarch, the Brother has been obligated.

G. W. P. I now invest you with the badge of Office, and proclaim you Worthy Associate of —— Division, No. —, •

for the present term. May you indeed prove a Worthy Associate, not only in honors, but in those qualities that adorn the highest station.

The Grand Conductor will escort the Brother to his station.

WORTHY PATRIARCH.

G. W. P. The Grand Conductor will now present to me the Worthy Patriarch elect.

G. C. Grand Worthy Patriarch, Brother ———, having been constitutionally exalted to the honorable station of Worthy Patriarch of this Division, is here respectfully presented for Installation.

G. W. P. Worthy Brother, you are now about to be inducted as the head of this Division—a station of trust, honor, and responsibility ; and when viewed as the free-will offering of your Brothers, it indeed affords a gratifying illustration of the position you hold in their confidence and esteem.

You will place your right hand on the left breast, while I administer the Obligation of your Office.

You solemnly and unreservedly pledge your sacred
. honor as a man, and as a Son of Temperance, in
presence of the Brothers here assembled, that you will
promptly and justly perform the duties of Worthy
Patriarch of this Division, to the best of your judgment
and ability, for the term of your election; during which
you will not permit any infringement on the Constitution
of the Grand Division, the Constitution and By-Laws of
this Division, or the Rules, Ceremonies, and Usages of
the Order of the Sons of Temperance—and that you will

at all times, to the utmost of your power, support the dignity of the Grand Division?

You furthermore pledge yourself, to allow none to visit this Division but Members thereof, without the Quarterly Password and Explanation,*—unless vouched for by a Brother in good standing—or the Traveling Password and Explanation, and the Entering Signal and Salutation—and that you will not countenance, directly or indirectly, or be present at the opening or session of any Division purporting to be Sons of Temperance, unless you are fully satisfied they are in possession of a legal and unforfeited Charter?

You furthermore pledge yourself, never to expose, or cause to be exposed, to any person not a Member of our Order, any part of the private books or papers intrusted to your care—that you will not take a copy of them, nor allow any other person so to do—that you will promptly deliver up the same, with all other property belonging to this Division in your possession or under your control, to your successor in Office, the Grand Worthy Patriarch, or his Deputy, when called upon so to do?

W. P. I do.

[*Three raps. G. W. P. proceeds.*]

Sharing the Confidence in your integrity and worth, of which the suffrage of your Brothers has given so distinguish-

---

* This shall not exclude Members of other Divisions who may be present at the opening of a Division, and able to give the Explanation to the Quarterly Password.—*Proceedings of National Division, June,* 1847.

ing an instance, it is with great satisfaction that I formally invest you with the badge of Office; and I now proclaim you Worthy Patriarch of —— Division, No. —, for the present term.

I also place in your possession the Charter of your Division—(*presents it*)—together with the Blue Books and other papers containing the private Forms and Ceremonies—(*presents them*)—and the Book of Constitutions—(*presents it*)—with a desire that you will make yourself thoroughly acquainted with each of them, to the end that innovation may be avoided, and the solemn Obligation you have this night, of your own free will and accord, taken upon yourself, sacredly maintained.

Lastly, Worthy Patriarch, I present you with the Gavel, an emblem of your authority—which it is hoped you will ever exercise with due prudence and brotherly regard. While decision and energy are highly desirable to your station, dignified and courteous demeanor is absolutely necessary to a proper and harmonious administration of the affairs of your Division.

Feeling assured that the direction of this Division is intrusted to good hands, I will now conduct you to your seat, and you will at once enter upon the arduous and responsible, yet honorable, duties of your Office.

[*Division sing :*]

> Whatever station we may hold
> Among the sons of earth—
> If high in honor, rich in gold,
> Or humble from our birth—

In VIRTUE only we behold
The standard of our worth,
Whatever station we may hold
Among the sons of earth.

[*One rap by W. P.*]

[*The W. P. can, if he wishes, address the Division.*

The G. W. P. gives the W. P. the new Password, etc. If there is any thing else to be communicated to the W. P. or to the Division, the G. W. P. does it here.]

G. C. Worthy Patriarch, you will please call up the Officers.

[*Two raps.*]

G. W. P. BROTHERS IN OFFICE : Into your keeping are intrusted matters of serious and weighty import—and a proper discharge of your respective duties will require the fullest exercise of your wisdom and vigilance. Your example can not fail to exert a powerful influence upon those around you, and it is therefore highly necessary that Candor, Uprightness, and Honor, should distinguish your actions, not only toward your Brothers, but toward the whole human race. Let the sentiment of the Ode we have just sung in harmony together, be impressed upon your minds— whatever station we may be called upon to fill, in VIRTUE only we behold the standard of our worth.

[*Three raps.*]

BROTHERS : The Officers of your choice are now in their places, and it is hoped and expected that their efforts to maintain good order and decorum, will receive your cheerful and prompt co-operation.

Never lose sight of the solemn Obligation you have taken to promote the harmony, advance the interest, and preserve unsullied, the reputation of the Sons of Temperance. Let the Emblem of our Order ever recall to your minds the three cardinal principles upon which our Institution rests, that the Star of Temperance may shine the brighter in the light of your virtues!

OFFICERS AND BROTHERS: Thanking you for your attention, we now take our leave.

[*The G. W. P. and G. C. will proceed to the center of the room and Salute the W. P. The Salutation is returned by the W. P. and all the Brothers. The Division remain standing until the Grand Officers have passed the Inside Sentinel.*]

INSTITUTING A NEW DIVISION.

*[New Divisions should be opened by the Grand Officers
when practicable. Sometimes, however, they are opened by
a single delegate, in which case he will administer the Obligation, and then proceed to the election of Officers.*

*If the Grand Officers officiate, they should be addressed by
their proper titles. If not, those who officiate should be
addressed as Officers of a Subordinate Division.*

*Open as a Subordinate Division, making such alteration
as the circumstances require, and omitting the Worthy Patriarch's charge to the Officers and Brothers.]*

[Three raps.]

G. W. P. We have met here this evening for the purpose
of diffusing the principles of Temperance and Benevolence.

[Division sing :]

> Yes, we in those principles join,
>> And such shall our actions display ;
> Our hands and our hearts shall combine
>> To extend their beneficent sway.
>
> Our laws we will ever respect,
>> Arise all contention above—
> And stand by each other erect,
>> In Purity, Friendship, and Love.

· *[One rap.]*

4

G. W. P. I now declare this meeting of the Sons of Temperance open for the purpose of Instituting ———— Division, No. —, of the Grand Division of the State of ————.

The Grand Conductor will see if the Applicants are ready.

[*The G. C. retires, and after ascertaining, returns and reports the names of those in waiting. If all correct, the G. W. P. says:*]

G. W. P. Some Brother will retire and introduce the Applicants to the Grand Conductor—after which let them be presented.

[*After the introduction, the Brother may return to the Division.*

When ready, the G. C. gives ONE *knock on the door, and directs the G. S. to announce that the Applicants are ready.*]

G. W. P. Admit them.

[*Three raps.*]

[*The G. C. leads the Applicants to the G. W. P.*]

G. C. Grand Worthy Patriarch, In obedience to your instructions, I here present (*read the names*), being the Applicants to the Grand Division of the State of ————, for a Charter to open ———— Division, No. —, of the Sons of Temperance.

G. W. P. Gentlemen (*or Brothers and Gentlemen, as may be*)—I have the pleasure of announcing that your application has been granted—and this evening we meet you for the purpose of organizing you as a Division. I will now claim your attention while the Grand Scribe reads the Charter, which will define your rights and privileges.

[*One rap.*]

[*The G. S. reads the Charter.*

If there are any who have not been Initiated, the G. W. P. says :]

G. W. P. Under this Charter, we will now proceed to Initiate those who are not Members of our Order.

[*The G. C. leads the Applicants who have not been Initiated, to the Ante-room.*

Let the Initiation follow, in the usual form, omitting the introduction to the A. C., as they have already been vouched for to the G. C., and making such other trifling alterations as may be necessary.

After the Initiation, let all the Applicants be presented.]

[*Three raps.*]

G W. P. By authority in me vested, I proclaim ——— Division, No—, of the Sons of Temperance, of the Grand Division of the State of ———, legally constituted ; and I now dedicate it to the cause of LOVE, PURITY, and FIDELITY.

[*Division sing :*]

> Our cause when first to light it burst,
>   Rear'd by a dauntless few,
> Appear'd so small, its early fall
>   Our foes prepared to view ;
> But more and more, from shore to shore,
>   Its influence shall extend,
> Our flag unfurl'd around the world,
>   Triumphant to the end.

Another band is reared to stand
  Among the brave array,
Before whose might, though hard the fight,
  Intemp'rance dies away ;
Our glorious plan to rescue man,
  From sorrow, vice, and shame,
Still gathers strength, until at length,
  May it the world reclaim !

G. W. P. Brethren—you are now fully empowered under this Charter, to perform all the Duties and Ceremonies of a Subordinate Division—and the Grand Division feels assured that in your keeping the Purity and Character of our Order will be fully sustained.

[One rap.]

[Proceed to the election of Officers.

Installation of Officers, according to form, with such alterations as may be necessary.]

NOTE.—In the addresses for the Opening of a Division, the presiding Officer is not confined strictly to those laid down, so long as the spirit is given.

FORMS FOR RECEIVING OFFICERS.

1. He directs the Inside Sentinel to announce him.

2. The Worthy Patriarch directs the acting Past Worthy Patriarch to retire and introduce him. As they enter, call up. They advance to the center of the room, the visitor salutes the Worthy Patriarch (right hand on the left breast), which is returned by the Worthy Patriarch.

3. The Division sing "Thrice welcome, Brother," or some other appropriate verse; during which the Past Worthy Patriarch escorts the visitor to the Past Worthy Patriarch's chair, that being a post of honor.

4. After the singing the Past Worthy Patriarch says:

Worthy Patriarch, Officers, and Brothers—I have the pleasure of presenting ——— ———, etc.

5. All place the right hand on the left breast, after which call down.

6. Should the Visitor RETIRE before the Division is regularly closed, he will advance to the center and Salute the Worthy Patriarch; the Division is called up, and the Salute

is returned by the whole. The Division will remain stand-ing until he passes the Inside Sentinel.

7. A Deputy simply visiting, or any other Official Visitor from the National, or a Grand Division, will be received in the same way—omitting to sing; but in the case of a Deputy visiting as an Installing Officer, the Division may sing or not, at its option.

A WORTHY PATRIARCH, OR PAST WORTHY PATRIACH, FROM ABROAD.

1. On his being announced, send out the Conductor to introduce him. They enter by the usual form. As he Salutes the Past Worthy Patriarch, call up the Division, and if thought proper, a verse may be sung.

2. The Conductor leads him to the front, and introduces him to the Worthy Patriarch, who extends a hand of wel-come ; he then introduces him to the Division—after which he is invited to a seat. Call down.

Note.—Perhaps nothing will tend to strengthen our Union more than paying suitable attention to visiting Brothers. It is therefore very desirable that those visits should be frequent, and rendered as agreeable and interesting as possible.

SUGGESTIONS AS TO THE MUSIC OF THE ORDER.

It is important, and pleasing as important, to have our Brotherhood everywhere use the same tunes.

The Committee, therefore, respectfully recommend the following airs to be sung:

OPENING.
(Old Tune:)
" Yes, we in those principles join,"

INITIATION.
(Sicilian Mariner's Hymn:)
" Traveler through a world of danger,"

(Shirland:)
" Blest be the tie that binds,"

(Mear:)
" Father of Mercies! condescend,"

(Old Hundred:)
" Spirit of love, benign and mild,"

(Old Lang Syne:)
"Once more we here the Pledge renew,"

CLOSING.
(Old Tune:)—No. 1.
" A goodly thing it is to meet,"

(Old Lang Syne:)—No. 2.
"Good-night, good-night to every one,"

NOTE.—When Initiation has preceded, it is suggested that No. 1 of the Closing Odes be sung, in order to vary the airs.

KEY.

29	27	34	15
A	B	C	D

19	20	56	91
E	F	G	H

41	13	16	48
I	J	K	L

25	32	22	37
M	N	O	P

18	11	62	75
Q	R	S	T

88	99	14	61
U	V	W	X

85	39
Y	Z

NOTE.—The above is the plan for transmitting the Passwords, etc. Each figure represents the letter immediately below it. For instance : Suppose the Password to be "Order," it would be written thus—22, 11, 15, 19, 11—and, by searching out the letter under each of these figures, the word is found.

DIAGRAM OF A DIVISION ROOM.

This page is intended to give an idea of the form of a Division, etc. The Room some-times will not allow the Officers to be placed as they are here, particularly the Sentinels. It is desirable, however, to conform as nearly as practicable.

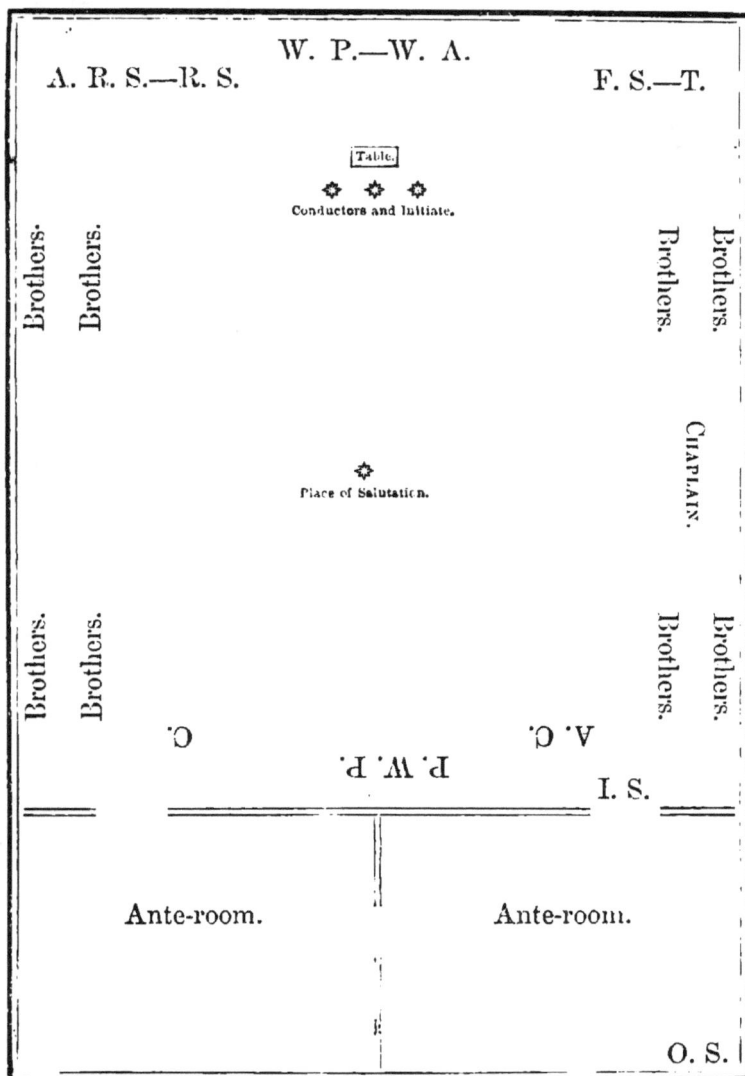

W. P.—W. A.

A. R. S.—R. S.   F. S.—T.

Table.

Conductors and Initiate.

Brothers. Brothers.   Brothers. Brothers.

CHAPLAIN.

Place of Salutation.

Brothers. Brothers.   Brothers. Brothers.

C.   A. C.

P. W. P.

I. S.

Ante-room.   Ante-room.

O. S.

www.ingramcontent.com/pod-product-compliance
Lightning Source LLC
Chambersburg PA
CBHW021540270326
41930CB00008B/1320